GROSS AND DISGUSTING JOBS

A Crabtree Branches Book

Julie K. Lundgren

CRABTREE
Publishing Company
www.crabtreebooks.com

School-to-Home Support for Caregivers and Teachers

This high-interest book is designed to motivate striving students with engaging topics while building fluency, vocabulary, and an interest in reading. Here are a few questions and activities to help the reader build upon his or her comprehension skills.

Before Reading:
- *What do I think this book is about?*
- *What do I know about this topic?*
- *What do I want to learn about this topic?*
- *Why am I reading this book?*

During Reading:
- *I wonder why...*
- *I'm curious to know...*
- *How is this like something I already know?*
- *What have I learned so far?*

After Reading:
- *What was the author trying to teach me?*
- *What are some details?*
- *How did the photographs and captions help me understand more?*
- *Read the book again and look for the vocabulary words.*
- *What questions do I still have?*

Extension Activities:
- *What was your favorite part of the book? Write a paragraph on it.*
- *Draw a picture of your favorite thing you learned from the book.*

TABLE OF CONTENTS

JOB HUNT

What do you want to do when you grow up? People do all kinds of work. Certain jobs require a bit of bravery and a strong stomach.

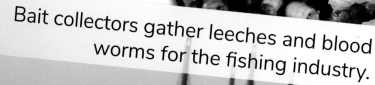

Bait collectors gather leeches and blood worms for the fishing industry.

4

Help Wanted:
Expert Sniffer
Odor testers smell new products.
Someone has to sniff armpits to see
if the deodorant is working!

Open wide!
Never trust a cat to tell you
how something tastes. Pet food
tasters make sure each new pet
food smells and tastes good.

Though difficult, we need people to do these important jobs. Jobs that are gross and disgusting to one person might not be to the right person. You might even find them interesting!

BLOOD, GUTS, MUSCLES, AND BONES

We rely on doctors, nurses, and other hospital workers to take care of us when things go wrong. **Surgeons** repair bodies of accident victims. Their skilled hands put pieces back in place like a living puzzle.

Surgeons make delicate and difficult repairs and are paid very well.

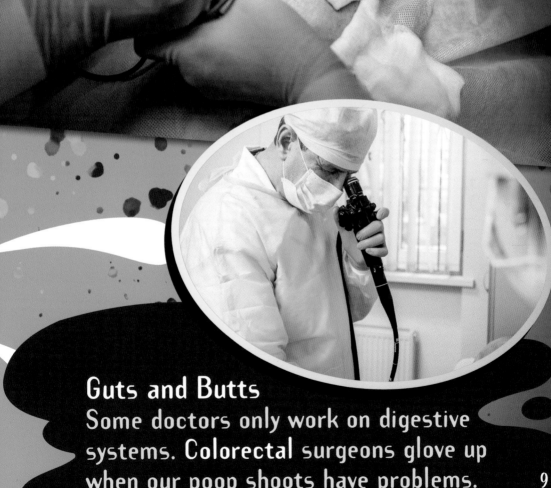

Guts and Butts
Some doctors only work on digestive systems. Colorectal surgeons glove up when our poop shoots have problems.

Wounds need cleaning. Nurses provide wound care by washing out smelly **pus**, blood, and dead skin regularly until the wound heals.

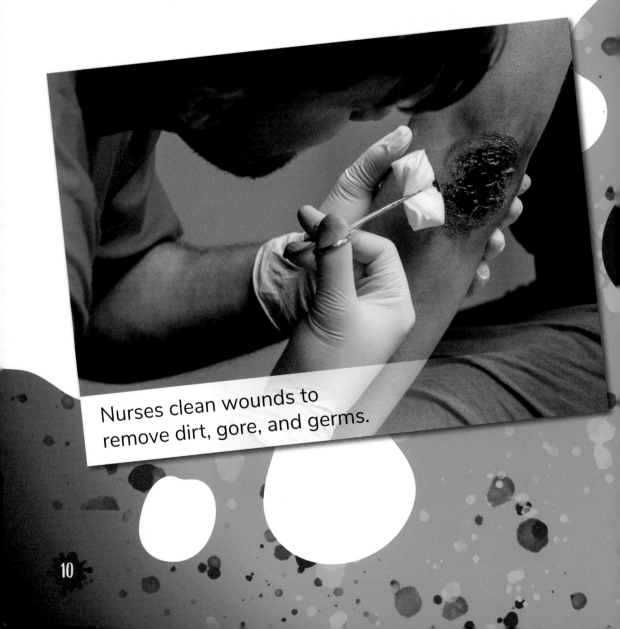

Nurses clean wounds to remove dirt, gore, and germs.

Medical Mess
After an operation, clinical waste technicians clear up all the extra parts, blood, and used gloves and gowns.

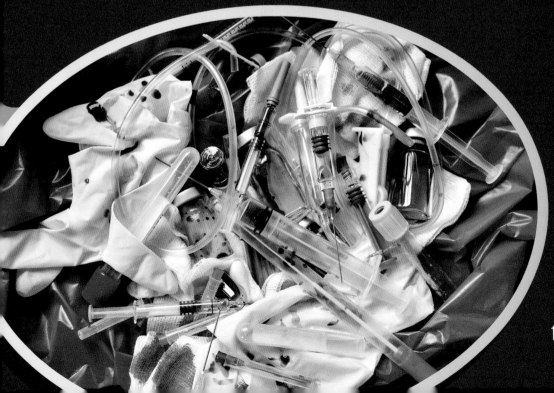

Dead bodies decay quickly. **Forensic pathologists** are doctors of the dead. They work to understand why someone died, by examining bodies inside and out. **Embalmers** clean and prepare bodies for burial.

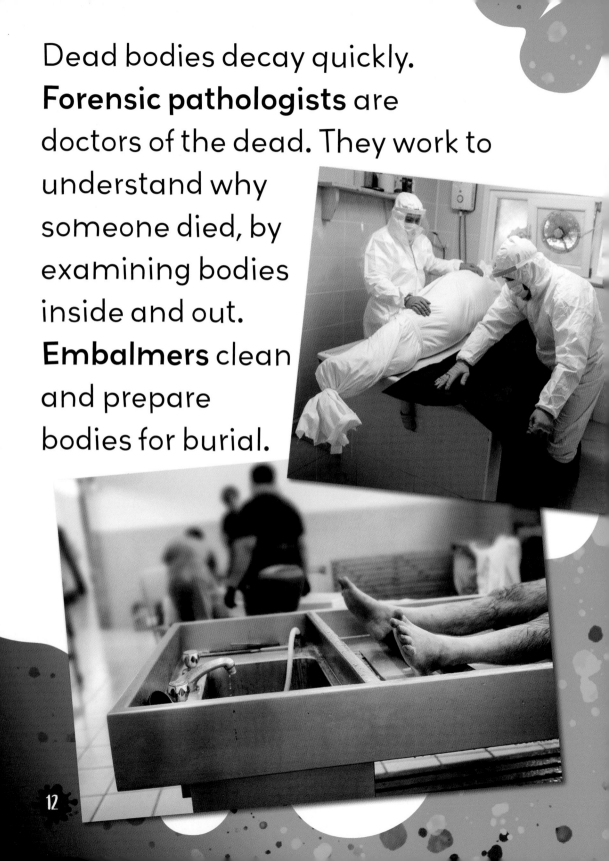

Mummies!
In ancient Egypt, embalmers had secret ways to preserve bodies of dead royalty and other important people.

13

MESS MANAGEMENT: POOP, PUKE, AND TRASH

We make messes every day. Who cleans up? **Sewage** systems need repairs. From the toilet to the treatment plant,

Sewage tank divers find and fix stinky problems.

plumbers and sewer workers keep sewage flowing.

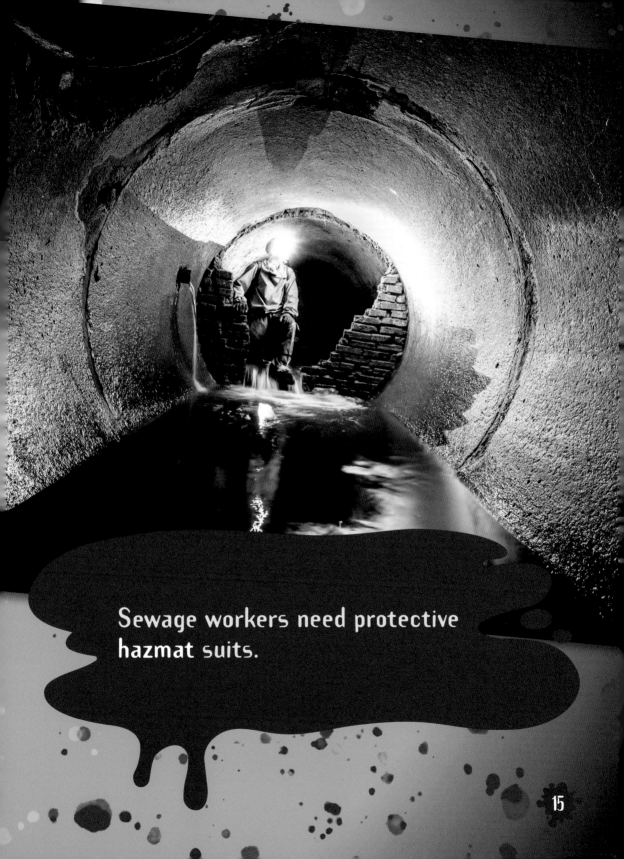

Sewage workers need protective hazmat suits.

Custodians keep our buildings clean and safe. Puke, pee, gum wads, and grime disappear thanks to them. Wet vacs suck up vomit in a flash.

Amusement parks hire vomit collectors for when riders get sick.

DO NOT CROSS

CRIME SCENE DO NOT CROSS

CRIME

Help Wanted: Crime Scene Cleaner
Beyond the yellow tape at a crime scene, cleaning crews clean up blood and gore left behind after investigators finish collecting evidence and clues.

Garbage smells of decay. Dirty diapers, used cat litter, decaying food, grease, and other waste make a stinky stew. After trucks collect your trash, waste workers sort it for processing.

Line workers pluck out harmful trash like batteries.

Food Recycling
Some schools and businesses send leftover food to farms as food for pigs.

CREEPY CRAWLY CAREERS

Do insects interest you? You may like to be a **forensic entomologist.** Flies lay eggs in dead things, including dead people. Forensic entomologists estimate when the person died based on how old the fly **larvae** are.

Insect experts consider temperature's effect on larvae growth.

This Is a Test

Companies developing mosquito repellent need product testers. Apply some repellent and see if the insects still find you tasty!

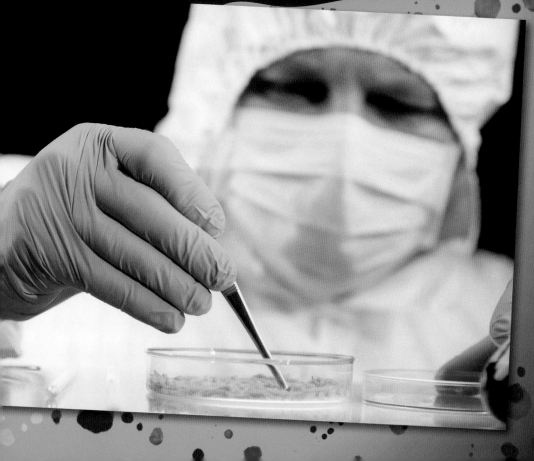

Exterminators get rid of mice, cockroaches, spiders, centipedes, snakes, and other house pests. They identify, track, and destroy unwanted guests.

Roaches in the house? Call an exterminator!

Rodent pest
control service

Home pest
insect control

Garden pest
control

I'D LIKE TO WORK WITH ANIMALS

Love animals? Veterinary technicians help with pet medical procedures. Could you swab goop, pus, ear wax, and live mites from an infested ear?

Veterinary technicians check poop samples for parasites.

Help Wanted:
Poop Checker
Manure inspectors collect and test samples of farm animal waste. They make sure it doesn't contain chemicals that might harm nearby land and water.

At meat processing plants, farm animals become food. Workers cut and package meat and other parts. They keep equipment, floors, and walls clean. From hoof to horn, everything gets used.

Meat processors wear protective gear.

Help Wanted: Poop Scooper

Gardeners prize bat **guano** to help plants grow. In underground caves, harvesters shovel guano toward a vacuum, which sucks it into a tank above ground.

Wildlife museum researchers may collect roadkill, noting animal type, date, size, location, and stomach contents. This information helps researchers understand more about animals, where they live, and what they eat.

Museum workers may make stuffed skins for lifelike displays.

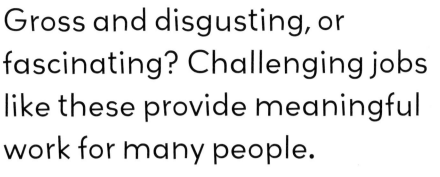

Gross and disgusting, or fascinating? Challenging jobs like these provide meaningful work for many people.

GLOSSARY

colorectal (koh-loh-RECK-tull): Having to do with the lower part of the digestive system

embalmers (em-BAL-merz): People who preserve and prepare bodies for burial

forensic entomologist (fer-EN-zick en-toh-MOLL-uh-jist): An insect scientist who specializes in determining time of death by studying insect development in dead bodies

forensic pathologists (fer-EN-zick path-OLL-uh-jists): Doctors who work to discover why someone died

guano (GWAH-no): Bat poop

hazmat (HAZ-mat): A short word for hazardous materials

larvae (LAR-vee): In insects, the stage of development between egg and adult

pus (PUSS): Thick, stinky fluid that oozes from infected wounds

sewage (SUE-widge): Human body waste, including poop and pee

surgeons (SER-junz): Highly trained doctors who perform difficult operations

technicians (tek-NIH-shunz): Trained people who do practical work or solve everyday problems

wounds (WOONDZ): Open cuts, tears, and scrapes on the body

INDEX

WEBSITES TO VISIT

www.batcon.org/article/guano-bats-gift-to-gardeners/

www.knowitall.org/series/kids-work

https://careerkids.com/pages/career-research

ABOUT THE AUTHOR
Julie K. Lundgren

Julie K. Lundgren grew up on the north shore of Lake Superior, a place of woods, water, and adventure. She loves bees, dragonflies, old trees, and science, and thinks parenting might also be a gross and disgusting job sometimes! Her interests led her to a degree in biology and a lifelong curiosity about wild places.

CRABTREE
Publishing Company

Produced by: Blue Door Education for Crabtree Publishing

Written by: Julie K. Lundgren

Designed by: Jennifer Dydyk

Edited by: Tracy Nelson Maurer

Proofreader: Crystal Sikkens

Cover splat art (on cover and throughout book) © SpicyTruffel page 4 (top) © NahomaLand, (bottom) © Cloud Yew, page 5 woman © Olena Zaskochenko, man © DWaschnig, page 6 bowl of food © Konstantin Faraktinov, scientist © Andrew Rybalko, cat with speech bubbles © KAMONRAT, page 7 © SatawatK, page 8 © Chaikom, page 9 (top) © Gerain0812, (bottom) © Roman Zaiets, page 10 © Photographee.eu, page 11 (top) © Tong_stocker, (bottom) © MAGNIFIER, page 12 (top) © Huseyin Aldemir, (bottom) © Giannis Papanikos, page 13 (top) © Cavan-Images, (bottom) © Andrea Izzotti, page 15 © Vladimir Mulder, page 16 © Robie Online, page 17 (top) © Tomacco, (bottom illustration) © chanwity, crime scene tape © Mega Pixel, page 18 workers © Photick, trash © DeawSS, page 19 (top) © riedjal, (bottom) © MagicBones, page 20 larvae © Astrid Gast, thermometer © meaculpa_1, page 21 (top) © Kwangmoozaa, (bottom) © StockMediaSeller, page 22 exterminator © Elnur, roaches © TIGER KINGDOM, rockes on backs © Rattiya Thongdumhyu, page 23 illustration © Visual Generation, rat © torook, page 24 © Adao, page 25 (top) © Fat Jackey, (bottom) © Igor Chus, page 26 © (top) © vodograj, (bottom) © TRphotomaker, page 27 (top) © Stephen Bonk, bats © Teguh Mujiono, (bottom) © sasimoto, page 28 (top) © NTL Photography, (bottom) © Nussar, page 29 © Brothers Art. All images from Shutterstock.com except cover © Photovs | Dreamstime.com, page 14 diver courtesy of U.S. Coastgard

Library and Archives Canada Cataloguing in Publication

Title: Gross and disgusting jobs / Julie K. Lundgren.
Names: Lundgren, Julie K., author.
Description: Series statement: Gross and disgusting things | "A Crabtree branches book". | Includes index.
Identifiers: Canadiana (print) 20210220406 | Canadiana (ebook) 20210220414 | ISBN 9781427154484 (hardcover) | ISBN 9781427154545 (softcover) | ISBN 9781427154606 (HTML) | ISBN 9781427154668 (EPUB) | ISBN 9781427154729 (read-along ebook)
Subjects: LCSH: Occupations—Juvenile literature. | LCSH: Occupations—Miscellanea—Juvenile literature. | LCSH: Job descriptions—Juvenile literature. | LCSH: Job descriptions—Miscellanea—Juvenile literature.
Classification: LCC HF5381.2 .L86 2022 | DDC j331.702—dc23

Library of Congress Cataloging-in-Publication Data

Names: Lundgren, Julie K., author.
Title: Gross and disgusting jobs / Julie K. Lundgren.
Description: New York, NY : Crabtree Publishing Company, [2022] | Series: Gross and disgusting things : a Crabtree Branches book | Includes index.
Identifiers: LCCN 2021022356 (print) | LCCN 2021022357 (ebook) | ISBN 9781427154484 (hardcover) | ISBN 9781427154545 (paperback) | ISBN 9781427154606 (ebook) | ISBN 9781427154668 (epub) | ISBN 9781427154729
Subjects: LCSH: Occupations--Juvenile literature. | Job descriptions--Juvenile literature.
Classification: LCC HF5381.2 .L86 2022 (print) | LCC HF5381.2 (ebook) | DDC 331.702--dc23
LC record available at https://lccn.loc.gov/2021022356
LC ebook record available at https://lccn.loc.gov/2021022357

Crabtree Publishing Company

www.crabtreebooks.com   1-800-387-7650

Printed in the U.S.A./072021/CG20210514

Published in the United States
Crabtree Publishing
347 Fifth Avenue, Suite 1402-145
New York, NY, 10016

Published in Canada
Crabtree Publishing
616 Welland Ave.
St. Catharines, ON, L2M 5V6